Morning Inspirations

Mark Dudley

iUniverse, Inc.
New York Bloomington

Morning Inspirations

iUniverse books may be ordered through booksellers or by contacting:

iUniverse
1663 Liberty Drive
Bloomington, IN 47403
www.iuniverse.com
1-800-Authors (1-800-288-4677)

ISBN: 978-1-4401-7414-8 (sc)
ISBN: 978-1-4401-7415-5 (ebk)

Printed in the United States of America

iUniverse rev. date: 9/23/2009

Words of Encouragement, Inspiring You to Pursue God's best.

"A Person who is progressively moving towards the accomplishment of a Dream or Goal is living the Ultimate Life"

Mark Dudley

Dedication

To my Lord and Savior Jesus Christ; I thank you and Give You All the Praise for What You've Done in My Life.

To My Three Daughters: Stacey, Victoria and Mckayla. Always know that I will always love you. Always strive to be the best in whatever you do!!

To my Mother: Mom, thank you for teaching me to trust God no matter what.

To Mychal, Randy, and Loretta: What more can I say but I Love You and I'm glad that you can witness what the Lord is doing with your little brother.

To all my friends: You have seen me in my good days and my dark days, and you were always there to encourage me. Thank You

To I-Universe Publishing: I'm so humbled that you allowed me to publish my books through you. Because of you I know I can share this gift with others.

SUCCESS QUOTES

“Success is not measured by what you accomplish but by the opposition you have encountered, and the courage with which you have maintained the struggle against overwhelming odds." **Orison Swett Marden**

"The truth of the matter is that there's nothing you can't accomplish if: (1) You clearly decide what it is that you're absolutely committed to achieving, (2) You're willing to take massive action, (3) You notice what's working or not, and (4) You continue to change your approach until you achieve what you want, using whatever life gives you along the way." **Anthony Robbins**

"Encouraged people achieve the best; dominated people achieve second best; neglected people achieve the least." Anonymous

"God put me on Earth to accomplish a certain number of things, Right now I'm so far behind I will never die” Anonymous

"If you don’t climb the mountain, you can’t view the plain." Anonymous

"Remember that great love and great achievements involve great risk." Anonymous

"The difference between the impossible and the possible lies in a person's determination." **Tommy Lasorda**

"Obstacles don't have to stop you. If you run into a wall, don't turn around and give up. Figure out how to climb it, go through it, or work around it." **Michael Jordon**

"When you know what you want, and you want it badly enough, you'll find a way to get it" **Jim Rohn**

"Follow your heart and your dreams will come true." **Anonymous**

"The ultimate victory in competition is derived from the inner satisfaction of knowing that you have done your best and that you have gotten the most out of what you had to give." **Howard Cosell**

DAY 1

Today's Topic: Independence Day
Scripture References: John 10:10; John 8:36

Success Quote: **"Winners dwell on and hold the self-image of that person they would most like to become. They get a vivid, clear, emotional, sensory picture of themselves as if they had already achieved their new role in life." Anonymous**

When you think of Independence Day you think of fireworks, hot dogs and a day at the beach. But true Independence comes when you know who you are in Christ and enjoy the life that has been provided for you through Jesus Christ. The word life means "**L**iving **i**n **F**ullness **E**veryday".

So many people even in the church are stressed out, frustrated, and overcome with worry when Jesus told us not to worry about tomorrow (Matthew chapter 6:33) and it could stem from the fact that they are not enjoying life.

I was reading a survey that said that many people are working at a job where they are underpaid, undervalued, and underappreciated but they would stay because the job is close to their house, or they won't give up their days off to start a new job. Our Heavenly Father has created a beautiful world for us to enjoy.

So enjoy what He has provided, and then you will have true Independence.

Day 2

Today's Topic: No Matter What
Scripture References: Romans 8:38-39, Philippians 4:13-14

Success Quote: **"If you are truly flexible and go until . . . there is really very little you can't accomplish in your lifetime." Anthony Robbins**

I was in the bookstore today buying one of my favorite magazine "Home-based Opportunities" when I saw the above titled book. The words "No Matter What" just seem to scream out at me, and I look at the title again and I realized that this is what the Lord would want us to do in our walk with Him.

All of us have experience times of great success, and times of distress. Even in those moments of despair when we felt like the whole world was against us, we continued to press onward.

I've always been impressed by the attitude of Warren Buffet, and Bill Gates; how they refused to let any disappointment stopped them in any business transactions.

We can look at Samson, David, and Peter and write sermons on how they failed God, but in the end they accomplished more for the Lord after their failure.

The Bible declares that the one that endures to the end shall receive a crown of life.

No Matter What means it doesn't matter what happened in my past or what is going on in my present I have a determination that nothing will stand in my way of walking in God's abundance.

No Matter What means is doesn't matter what people have said about me or done to me I've come too far by faith to turn around now. And the mere fact that I'm going through so much is because God is preparing me for my hundred-fold harvest.

So I would say to you my friends that Your Best Days and Your Bless Days Are Just Ahead of You Just Keep The Faith And ***No Matter What*** Be Fully Persuaded That What God Has Spoken Over Your Life Will Come To Pass!!

DAY 3

Today's Topic: Trusting God
Scripture References: Proverbs 3:5

Success Quote: **"When I've heard all I need to make a decision, I don't take a vote. I make a decision." Ronald Reagan**

Many people believe in God, but not many believe God. One of the most incredible places that we can live our lives is in the continual position of believing God. God made us, and God is able to empower us to do what He calls us to do. The person that puts God first will find God with him right up to the end. "In everything you do, put God first. He will direct you and crown your efforts with success" (Proverbs 3:6, TLB).

God never made a promise that was too good to be true. One of the great things about believing God is found in Luke 18:27 "The things which are impossible with men are possible with God". When you join together with Him in His plan, things that were impossible now become possible.

The superior man seeks success in God. The small man seeks success in himself and others. You will never tap God's resources until you have attempted the impossible. Great things are achieved by those who dare to believe that the God inside them is superior to any circumstance. If you dream big, believe big, and pray big, do you know what will happen? Big Things!!

Dare to go with God farther than you can see, Psalm 84:11 declares "No good thing will He withhold from them who walk uprightly". A small man stands on others. A great man stands on God. Trust Him because He will never, ever fail you!

DAY 4

Today Topic: God's Chandelier
Scripture References: Eph 2:10, Matthew 5:16

Success Quote: **"Before you can inspire with emotion, you must be swamped with it yourself. Before you can move their tears, your own must flow. To convince them, you must yourself believe."**

Winston Churchill

We have in our church a beautiful chandelier, and it's positioned high above in the center of the sanctuary. Now the chandelier is not one big light, but it's a combination of one big light along with about 20 or 30 lights or what is called ***Votives***. Each of these ***Votives*** play a very important part in making this chandelier look so beautiful that people are amazed by it's beauty.

The above scripture tells us to let our light so shine before men that they may see our good works and Glorify the Father which is in Heaven. This means that you and I are the ***Votives*** in the redemption plan of God. We must shine the light of His presence everywhere we go. This light is to dispel all the darkness that we see in our families, and community, to show them there's a better way to go, and that's there's more to this life than what they are doing now. This light is to shine when we go to our different occupations where people are concerned about job security, we should be the one that walks in the peace of God; trusting Him to meets all our needs.

We are the ***Votives*** that are not ashamed to step out of the "box" and go where no man has gone before, and to believe for what seem impossible. Never allow what is happening around you change what is happening on the inside of you.

You are just as important in the eyes of God as your pastor, or anyone else you may see stand in front of the congregation. They may not mention your name, or recognize you, or even thank you for your service, but know that there's someone either in your family, or on your job that see's the Glory of God shining through you.

In God's Chandelier you are His ***Votives*** letting the world know that Jesus is the Answer.

DAY 5

Today Topic: Stretch Yourself
Scripture: Mark 9:23

Success Quote: **"If you don't climb the mountain, you can't view the plain." Anonymous**

I love reading magazines on the success stories of millionaires. Each story is different but it has the same message. In one magazine they were interviewing Richard Branson the owner of Virgin Atlantic Airlines, and he shared one of the secrets of his success: You must be willing to make a fool of yourself.

Now I want to simplify that response by saying this: You'll never unleash your potential and reach your goals in life if you don't STRETCH YOURSELF.

If you examine the relationship that Jesus had with his disciples, He was always exhorting them to do something outside the norm. One example is when He (Jesus) was walking on the water and He bid Peter to come to him. Many people are looking for their ship to come in instead of swimming out to it.

To do something great, you must first become uncomfortable. Uncomfortable always comes before comfortable. Tiger Woods, Michael Dell, Warren Buffet all stretched themselves, they took risks, they had the courage to preserve and now their enjoying the reward for their willingness to stretch themselves.

Let me pose this question: What is the one thing you desire in life that you know will "push" you, whatever it is don't be afraid to go for it. With God on your side the possibilities are unlimited.

You don't have to stretch yourself 100% or 50%, just 10% and let God open the windows of heaven and pour out a blessing that you won't have room enough to contain it.

DAY 6

Today Topic: The Law of Displacement
Scripture Reference: Matthew 12:35

Success Quote: **"Outstanding leaders go out of their way to boost the self-esteem of their personnel. If people believe in themselves, it's amazing what they can accomplish." Sam Walton**

The Law of Displacement-Whatever enters me determines what exits me.

There's a show on television called CSI: Miami, it centers on crime scene investigators who uses science to solve crimes. I was watching one particular episode that really caught my attention. There were a group of teenagers acting out what they have seen in a video game that depicted acts of violence. Most recently another teenager confessed that he acted out a crime based on a character he saw in the movies. I've heard of many people who watched the wrestling show "Smack down" who have used the same wrestling maneuvers on their friends with sometime tragic results.

The Bible tells us to be mindful of what we allow our ears to hear, and what comes before our eyes (Proverbs 4:22-23). Joshua 1:8 gives us the secret to success in our walk with the Lord: Mediate in the book of the Law on a consistent basis, and observe or act upon all that is written in the word. James 1:15 tells us to be "doers" or "imitators of the Word of God.

As we all press towards the mark for the prize of the high calling of God, it's critical that we don't allow anything negative to stop our progress. We must ignore those who attempt to tell us how far we can go in life, and keep our eyes looking to the hills from where our help comes from.

Stay focus. Fill your heart (spirit) and mind with the Word of God everyday for there is life and success to those who attend to the Word.

DAY 7

Today Topic: People Worship-An Enemy to your success
Scripture References: Exodus 32:21, 2 Samuel 15:24

Success Quote**: "Far too many people have no idea of what they can do because all they have been told is what they can't do. They don't know what they want because they don't know what is available for them" Zig Ziglar**

The above two scriptures details the story of Aaron, and King Saul, both these men instead of following the commandments of God gave in to people pressure with dire consequences.

I was in church Sunday leading Praise and Worship, and I was ministering a worship song that spoke of how deeply we need The Lord. As I was singing the song I closed my eyes and began to cry out to God how much I needed him. I was so into the song I totally forgot the people in the congregation; it was as if I was standing before the throne of God kneeling before Him with tears streaming down my face in absolute reverence to Him. He spoke these words to me that was so clear and so profound: People Worship Is an Enemy to Your Success.

I mediated on those words as He reminded me of Aaron, and King Saul. People worship will hinder your progress in God. Our acceptance does not come from people but it comes from the One who created us on purpose for a purpose. When we look to people to validate us, we give them control on who we are, and how far we can go in God.

Many people in the body of Christ have gifts and talents lying dormant for fear of people's reaction. We must not be moved by the opinions of others, but be totally dependant on the Spirit of God to lead us to where God has already prepared for us to go.

Don't allow anyone to stand in the way of your harvest. Your Heavenly Father knows you better than anyone and He looks at you and says "I'm Proud of You".

Day 8

Today Topic: The Attitude of "Never"
Scripture Reference: 2 Corinthians 4: 8-15-18, Isaiah 43-18-19, Psalm 91:1, Philippians 1:6

Success Quote: **"No man is ever whipped, until he quits -- in his own mind." Napoleon Hill**

The Attitude of "Never" is a powerful success principle that is being used by successful people everywhere.

Donald Trump is a billionaire real-estate developer. In his many years of business he has suffered some financial loss. He declared bankruptcy, and had to close down some of his businesses, but He has never stop building new condominiums. He has seen the fruit of this attitude and now has made more money than he could imagine.

This is the Attitude God the Father desire for his children to have. I want to share these truths with you, and it's my prayer that you would apply them to your life.

First, I want to give you the Webster definition of Never: An adverb; a declaration that something will not happen.

(1) Never let your present circumstances hinder you from pursuing God's best.

2 Corinthians 8:15-16, Psalms 37:25

(2) Never let your past decisions determine your future outcome.

Isaiah 43:19, 2 Corinthians 5:17

(3) Never let anyone question the extent of your relationship with God.

Psalms 91:1, Matthew 6:6

(4) Never Give Up

Philippians 1:6, Galatians 6:9

(5) Never forget The Lord has promised never to leave you nor fail you.

Joshua 1:7, Hebrews 13:6

DAY 9

Today Topic: It shall come to Pass
Scriptures References: Romans 4:17-18, Mark 11:24, Ephesians 4:23

Success Quote: " **I am still determined to be cheerful and happy, in whatever situation I may be; for I have also learned from experience that the greater part of our happiness or misery depends upon our dispositions, and not upon our circumstances." Martha Washington**

God spoke to a man named Noah, and told him to build an ark because there was a flood coming. The flood didn't come the next day, month, or year but it did come.

God spoke to Abraham and told him he would be a father of a son. Abraham was about 100 years old, and his wife Sarah was not too far behind him in age, but the baby was born.

Jesus told the religious leaders He would rise again after they crucified Him, and in three days He got up with all power in His Hands!!

The point that I'm trying to convey to you is this: Whatever God has spoken over your life rest assured It Shall Come to Pass. I was just sitting at my desk and I was encouraging myself with these scriptures.

Because I believe God for yours and my business to take off, and our finances to be blessed so that we can leave an inheritance for our children's children, and for the assignment He has called us to. There are times I can be the worse patient in the world. And the worse patient is someone who is impatient and anxious. I felt that way, and God has to remind me that His Word will not return to Him void, but it shall accomplish what He Has designed.

I sense this so strongly in my spirit that there are many of you who feel the same way, and I want to tell you Don't Give up on God for He Won't Give up on you!! Whatever He Promise You Can Believe It Shall

Come To Pass!! Keep Praying, Keep Believing and Keep Expecting Because God watches Over His Word to Perform It!!

Day 10

Today Topic: Be At Rest
Scripture References: Matthew 6:30-33, 1 Peter 5:7

Success Quote: "**Where there is no struggle, there is no strength**."
Oprah Winfrey

Like many of you I have some struggles and battles that I'm facing. Sometimes these battles can be so stressful that you wonder "Where is God". With the word "recession" becoming the new catch phrase it's refreshing to know that we have a Jehovah-Jireh who will provide.

The Lord has a way of speaking to me through a song and the song "Be at Rest" came up in my spirit. The song reminds us of what the Lord has done for us; how He has delivered you from your past, and had protected you and provided for you. As I meditated on this song I thought about you my friends, and I want to encourage your hearts today.

(1) ***Be at Rest Knowing the Plan of God will be fulfilled.***
Jeremiah 29:11, Philippians 1:6

(2) ***Be at Rest knowing that God has forgiven you.***
1 John 1:9, Psalms 103:12

(3) ***Be at Rest Knowing That God has heard Your Prayers***
Mark 9:23, Matthew 7:7

(4) ***Be at Rest knowing that someone is Praying for You***

That someone is me. I believe that God has His Hand of Favor and Increase on your life. You will be all that He created you to be.

DAY 11

Today's Topic: The Voice
Scripture Reference: Psalms 29:4-8

Success Quote: **You are what you are and where you are because of what has gone into your mind. You can change what you are and where you are by changing what goes into your mind" Zig Ziglar**

How powerful is the voice of the Lord. The Bible declares there are many voices in the world, and we hear them everyday proclaiming doom and gloom. It's interesting to me that people are so quick to listen to the voices of negativity (swine flu, and recession) but attack those who speak words of comfort and hope.

I was in the bookstore recently and saw a book with a title that really surprised me. The book was title "A Child called it" and it was based on a true story. I read just a few pages and could only imagine what this child went through being called an "It", and I thought back to how many times I heard people tell me that someone told them "They weren't good enough, or smart enough, or remind them of things they have done". I would always asked them where is the person that said this to them, and they would call out someone name. I then would say I don't physically see them, and tell them that they have allowed that voice of "you can't, and "you're not good enough" become so dominated that now they themselves are repeating it and it's causing them to believe what was said.

Proverbs 18:21 tells us that death and life are in the power of the tongue and they that love it shall eat the fruit thereof (whether it's death or life). The purpose behind the consistent study of the Word of God is to become more acquainted with the Voice of The Lord as He speaks to us through His Word. The Voice of the Lord tells us that we are the apple of His eyes, The Voice of The Lord tells us that we the Head and not the Tail, The Voice of The Lord tells us that He has designed us to increase and have abundant Life.

What You Hear determines How You Feel. Learn to Hear the Voice of The Lord because He wants to Lead You to your wealthy Place

DAY 12

Today Topic: Seize Your Day
Scripture Reference: Ecclesiastes 3: 1-8

Success Quote: **"The price of success is hard work, dedication to the job at hand, and the determination that whether we win or lose, we have applied the best of ourselves to the task at hand." Vince Lombardi**

In sports there are different seasons. We experience seasonal changes in the weather every year. In every season there are lessons that are learned, and challenges that are met.

Many of us have experience seasons of failure and lost whether in relationships, or financially, but we learned some very important life lessons even when it seemed that nothing was going right.

I believe in my spirit that we are now in a new season where God is blessing us beyond what we can ask or imagine. It is essential that we seize this time. If you obey all the rules, you miss all the fun.

Your current safe boundaries were once unknown frontiers. A ship that stays in the harbor is safe, but that is not what ships are built for. You were created to increase, to abound, to go higher, and to do more. If your ship doesn't come in, swim out to it.

Twenty years from now you will be disappointed by the things you didn't do than by the ones you did. So throw off the bowlines. Sail away from the safe harbor. Catch the trade winds in your sails.

You can't do anything about the length of your life, but you can do something about its width and depth. The road to success is lined with many tempting parking spaces. Anyone who thinks the sky is the limit has limited imagination.

Some make it happen, some watch it happen, and some say, "What Happened?" Every man dies, not every man lives. To make changes your life: Start immediately. Do it flamboyantly. No exceptions. You may delay, but time will not.

A wise man makes good decisions. Others follow people's opinions. This is your season Seize it and enjoy what the Lord has given you.

Day 13

Today's Topic: You are destined to Win
Scripture Reference: Psalm 119:105

Success Quote**: "Winning is everything, to win is all there is. Only those poor souls buried beneath the battlefield understand this**." **SEAL Team Saving**

I was reading a story about an airline pilot who was going through some rough weather condition. The pilot shared that he was always taught three important lessons: (1) Always maintain constant communication with the control tower; (2) Listen for instructions from the control tower on how to get through the rough weather; and (3) Always remember what was taught to them out of their manual.

As I read this story it really brings the above scripture to life for me. No matter what storm you may be facing:(1) Keep in constant contact with your Heavenly Father (Psalms 23:1-2); (2) Listen for the still small voice of the Holy Spirit leading and guiding you (Romans 8:14); (3) Always remember God's word says No weapon formed against you will prosper!!

Storms come to every one of us, and sometimes it feels like those storms lasts a lifetime, but here's some good news: Champions are the ones who endure the storm and never quit. Yes you may feel like giving up which is human nature but remember our example Jesus Christ who for the joy that was set before endure the cross, and now He's seated at the right hand of the Father making intercession for you and me. I want to tell you that you can't give up now; you've come too far to quit.

You are destined by God to overcome every challenge, every battle, and every storm. Be strong In the Lord and In the Power of His Might

Day 14

Today's Topic: God Favors You
Scripture References: Psalm 30:5, Deuteronomy 1:11

Success Quote: "**The Lord gives us a plan to follow. It is outlined in His commandments. And all those commandments are designed to build stability within us. We are not to excuse our failures and weaknesses: We are not to say we are made the way we are, and thereby justify our sins. The Lord expects us to rise above our weakness, become strong, and pattern ourselves after Him" Anonymous**

What a great and mighty God we serve. With all that is happening in the world today, it's so good to know that God Favor is Upon Us.

Many of us have been through so much but yet God has provided for us. We can all testify how we were the least likely to succeed in our family but God has blessed us beyond our imagination.

The Bible records many stories of God's Favor: David being chosen as King of Israel over his brothers, Joseph gaining favor to see the King even though he was in prison, Ruth being chosen as Boaz's wife even though she was a Moabite.

It's so wonderful to know that His Favor is being revealed in our lifetime as well. Many of us have lost jobs but still God provided. Some of us have made some bad decisions financially but God has still supplied every one of your needs. So many are fearful and worried about what they see or read in the newspapers, but isn't it amazing that even in what the world says is difficult financial times the people of God is experiencing His Favor on a even greater scale.

I encourage you everyday to Thank God for His Favor being upon you. You're His Favorite Son or Daughter. You are the apple of His eyes, His prized creation!!

Day 15
Today Topic: The Other One
Scripture References: Isaiah 55:8; 1 Corinthians 1:20

Success Quote: "**A true leader has the confidence to stand alone, the courage to make tough decisions, and the compassion to listen to the needs of others. He does not set out to be a leader, but becomes one by the equality of his actions and the integrity of his intent." Douglas McCarther**

In my study of the Word of God today I discovered something quite interesting. God always uses the one that people have ignored or disqualified.

In Genesis Abraham's father was on the border of Canaan but it was Abraham that actually went into the Promised Land.

In the Book of Esther, Boaz could have picked anyone to be his wife, but he chose Ruth a Moabite.

In the book of Samuel the prophet was looking to anoint the next king of Israel. He came to Jesse who brought all his sons, and the prophet asked Jesse if he had anymore sons, and Jesse said there was one more but he was out in the field. Jesse didn't see the potential in his own son, many people failed to see your potential but He who began a good work in You Will Finish the Work He Started(Phil 1:6). When David the Other One showed up The Prophet saw the kingly anointing on David.

It was the Other One Joseph who was thrown in a pit by his own brothers, taken to Egypt, imprisoned for a crime he did not commit that would save his family during a time of famine.

In the New Testament many people thought John the Baptist was the messiah, but John said there is someone coming whose shoes I cannot fit, and The Other One was Jesus Christ who died for our sins, but rose again and in now making intercession for you and me.

The Other One was the Apostle Paul who watched as Stephen was stoned to death, who wrote most of the New Testament who said that He fought a good fight, and have kept the faith.

You might be the Other One; the one people ignore and push aside. You might be the Other One, the one people always look at based on your mistakes or inadequacy as "no good". I have good news God always uses The Other One to accomplish great things. Because you stood on His Word, and made tough choices, and refuse to back down this is your due season to be bless beyond what you can ask or think!!

Day 16

Today's Topic: The Law of Eventuality
Scripture Reference: Galatians 5:6-8

Success Quote: **"I found every single successful person I've ever spoken to had a turning point. The turning point was when they made a clear, specific unequivocal decision that they were not going to live like this anymore; they were going to achieve success. Some people make that decision at 15 and some people make it at 50, and most people never make it all" Brian Tracy**

Every decision has a consequence whether good or bad. We see that every time they show people who for years smoked cigarettes, or drank alcohol. It saddened me when I hear about another teenager losing his or her life as a result of driving while intoxicated in spite of the many warnings.

The Law of Inevitability is based on the information we are hearing, the people we listen to, and the environment we're in. I've seen many young people who were raised by good parents get caught up in gangs because of the environment they are around, and the negative voices they hear from their friends.

Many young teenage girls play a very dangerous game with their bodies only to inevitably become pregnant before they finish school (I watch Maury Povich and it's sickens me). But with every negative there is a positive.

The Law of Inevitability is a powerful success principle that when used from a biblical standpoint is critical to our success. The Bible declares that when we seek the Lord He will answer (Jeremiah 33:1). Faith comes when we hear the Word of God (Romans 4:17). When we give, it is given unto us good measure press down and shaken together (Luke 6:38). When we confess our sins He is Faithful and Just to Forgive(1 John 1:9) And here is the most powerful part of this principle: When we seek The Lord and His Kingdom and His Righteousness(His way of doing things) everything we desire shall be added unto us(Matthew 6:33).

Understand the Law of Inevitability because it will lead you to your wealthy place in Jesus Name.

DAY 17

Topic: He Will Keep His Word
Scripture Reference: Psalm 138:8

Success Quote: **"No matter how steep the mountain - the Lord is going to climb it with you" Helen Steiner Rice**

The above scripture is one of my favorites in the Bible. It reminds us that whatever is a concern for us is a concern of our Heavenly Father. Your situation did not catch God by surprise. He's well aware of what you're facing and He has already provided a way out for you. It may seem like you're in a storm but know that Jesus is in the boat with you, not just to calm the storm, but comfort you through it. I've quoted this scripture many times when I had no food or money, and it seemed like my friends had joined the witness protection program because I couldn't find them.

I believe that my assignment is to encourage the saints that the plan of God will be accomplish in their lives. You were created to have dominion and to experience increase and growth in your life. God has never and nor will He ever fail you. So whenever you're facing a problem turn your face from the problem and turn your eyes upon Jesus. God's word will not return to him void but it will accomplish that which He has promised.

DAY 18

Today's Topic: Confidence
Scripture Reference: Philippians 4:13, Isaiah 46: 3, 4

Success Quote: **"Success is the ability to go from one failure to another with no loss of enthusiasm" Sir Winston Churchill**

The Apostle Paul was beaten down constantly and brought into impossible situations. He despaired of his life. Yet Christ kept raising him up. Resurrection life proceeds from such crucifixion. Paul can attest to that fact that no matter what the situation God was able to deliver. Paul shared this confidence in the above scripture that He can do all things through Christ that strengthen him. He did not rely on his own strength or ability or inability but rested in this awareness that based on his relationship with the Lord that God was bigger than any problem he faced. And it didn't matter what it was it would not hinder him from completing his assignment for the Lord.

We must have this same kind of confidence in God, that whatever I'm facing I'm not facing it alone. As a matter of fact while the problem is facing us, we should keep our eyes on Jesus the author and finisher of our faith. There are several keys to building this confidence in God:

(1) ***Recognize that your heavenly Father wants good things to happen for you***: James 1:17

(2) ***Associate with people who will keep your fire burning***
"He that walks with wise men shall become wise" Proverbs 24:11

(3) ***Fill every conversation with Faith talk***. Words matter. They move you toward your dream or away from it. Your words should continuously reflect your total confidence in the God you serve.

(4) ***Keep Your Song of Praise on your lips***. There's one song that moves you into the presence of God and reminds you of his provision, and delivering power.

As you build your confidence in God you'll know beyond any doubt that he will see you through.

DAY 19

Today Topic: Endurance
Scripture Reference: Hebrews 11: 1-40, 1 Corinthians 9:24

Success Quote: **"Having chosen our course, without guile and with pure purpose, let us renew our trust in God, and go forward without fear and with manly hearts." Abraham Lincoln.**

Abraham, Enoch, Noah, Gideon, and Samson, All these men and others are mentioned in Hebrews chapter eleven which is called "The Hall of Fame of Faith". They were placed there because they dare to trust God to fulfill His Word.

They faced many obstacles, and some have experienced periods of failures and rejection but they overcame and completed God's divine purpose.

Every great champion in Biblical history had to endure different seasons in their lives. Moses the great man who led Israel out of bondage overcame his inability to speak fluently. David overcame being the last one to be seen by the prophet who upon seeing him anointed him the next king of Israel.

Obstaçles are unavoidable but are necessary in the process of completing the will of God.

A mountain climber encountered many things while they are heading towards the top of the mountain, but their focus is not on the pain or the cold weather but on reaching the peak of the mountain.

Oral Roberts the great healing evangelist overcame stuttering and tuberculosis to begin a ministry that touched many lives and helped mentored other well-known ministries.

The Bible declares that the one who wins the race is the one who keeps running, so yes there are hurdles to jump over and mountains to climb but the end result is hearing the Lord says "Well done".

DAY 20
Today Topic: Life Lessons
Scripture Reference: Proverbs 3:5

Success Quote**: "I've failed over and over and over again in my life and that's why I succeed" Michael Jordan**

I entitled this Life lessons because I believe everyday were learning something new. I've learned that Life is a collection of decisions that determine the joy or pain we experience.

Today I took a test in school, and I've been studying for this test for the last two weeks, and I was ready for it to be over. I was handed the test material and sat there totally confused. I've studied only one portion of the test material instead of studying all the material. I failed by only seven points and have to take the test over again.

I walked out of the class disappointed in myself and once again the pity party was ON!!

I got on the train and wondered what happened. I thought I was ready to pass this test, and I looked up and saw three big words on this poster: Get over It!!

I sat there looking at this sign and the Holy Spirit began to speak to me asking "What did you learn from this, what will you do the next time this occurs", but it wasn't just this test but Life in general.

We've all had disappointments and failures in our lives, and yes they hurt but within every disappointment there is a lesson to be learned. I learned that God not only wants us to be blessed financially, but also in our relationship with our children and spouses.

I've learned that God not only desire for us to have a strong prayer life, and know all the Hebrew translation of every word in the Bible, but He also wants us to witness to the lost, and hurting in our families and communities.

So if you feel like you're in a storm whether it's a storm of fear, and uncertainty look for the life lesson in the storm that will take you to your next level in God.

DAY 21

Today's Topic: Passion
Scripture Reference: Philippians 3:13-14

Success Quote: **Don't aim for success if you want it; just do what you love and believe in and it will come naturally" David Frost**

Passion is power. Passion is desire. It includes the desire to change, serve, or achieve a goal.

People who are succeeding greatly possess great passion. They are consumed and obsessed. It burns within them like fire. Nothing matters to them but the completion of the instructions of God in their lives.

Henry Ford had a passion when it came to automobiles. Thomas Edison for inventions. The Wright Brothers for the airplanes.

Isaiah was passionate. "For the Lord God will help me, therefore I will not be confounded, therefore I have set my face like a flint, and I know I shall not be ashamed,"(Isaiah 50:7)

We see the passion of the Apostle Paul in the above mentioned scripture.

Jesus Christ had a passion for His mission and goal in life (Luke 19:10, and Acts 10:38) His passion for the salvation of mankind took him to the cross (Hebrews 12:2)

We are instructed by God to develop a passion for the Word of God (Joshua 1:8, Proverbs 4: 3-4).

Passion is the difference between those who start and finish, and the one who give up.

Be passionate about your relationship with the Lord. The Bible says that the one who ask, seek, and knock will be the one who sees doors open unto them.

Be passionate when it comes to standing on His Word even when it looks like nothing is happening because God watches over His Word to perform it.

The people who know their purpose have passion. And the people who know their purpose and have passion are the ones who prosper.

Let us be the people who prosper because we have a passion to see the Lord be Lifted up That He May Draw All Men unto Him!!

DAY 22

Today Topic: Consistency
Scripture Reference:

Success Quote: "**The ladder of success is best climbed by stepping on the rungs of opportunity" Avn Rand**

Consistency-The ability to maintain a particular standard or repeat a practice with minimal variation.

Daniel prayed three times daily. David prayed seven times. Jesus always returned to the synagogue and to be taught.

Dustin Hoffman one of the most well known actors of our time was nominated for the Academy Award on five different occasions but never won, so did Martin Scorsese who directed many of the classic movies of our time. Both these men finally won. Michael Jordan didn't win his first championship ring until his seventh year in the NBA, but he kept on playing until he did.

The difference between the one who is successful and the one who isn't is that one continues doing what they love to do in spite of the obstacles and challenges they faced, while the other gives up when they don't see instant results, or the pressures of life zaps their enthusiasm.

I've seen many in the church start off serving God with zeal, and a fire that last until the storms of life come and they become weary in well doing.

I've witnessed people wanting to start a business, or play an instrument start off great, but ended up giving up their dream.

Consistency means that I won't move by external circumstances. I have set my heart to follow the principles of God that are essential to my success in life.

Quoting from the song: He's able: "Don't give up on God because He won't give up on you!

Day 23

Today's Topic: Expectation
Scripture Reference: Mark 11:24

Success Quote: "Nobody is stronger; nobody is weaker than someone who came back. There is nothing you can do to such a person because whatever you could do is less than what has already been done to him. We have already paid the price" Elie Wiesel

What is your expectation?

The Bible says that God does exceedingly; abundantly above all we can ask or think, so God always operates from the standpoint of doing things on a larger scale.
In Genesis God told Abraham to leave his country, and his family and go to our land that He would show him.

He spoke to Moses and told him to take the people across to the other side before the red sea was opened.

He told Joshua to tell the people to walk around the wall of Jericho for seven days, and on the seventh day shout!!

Jesus told his disciples to go to the upper room and wait until they were filled with the Holy Ghost.

We can tell from these examples that the Lord will always do something out of the ordinary, and that should be our mindset. Our expectation of ourselves, and our dreams, and goals should be higher.

Les Brown said "People don't succeed because they aim high and miss, but because they aim low and hit". Raise the level of your expectations. Don't just believe to able to pay your mortgage, but believe that you'll be able to pay someone else mortgage as well. Don't accept being an employee but believe to be an employer.

Life is no rehearsal. You have one chance, so why not expect the best for you and your family. We serve a big God who desires us to have always an abundance mentality.

So raise your level of expectation because the God we serve is more than able to supply all your needs!!

DAY 24

Today Topic: Change Your Seat
Scripture Reference: Ephesians 2: 6-7

Success Quote: "Always live life in the forward motion, never in reverse" Mark Dudley

Now many of us have been on an airplane. And every aircraft has two sections: First Class, and Coach. Now in coach you have to share your seat with almost anyone, and sometimes that could be very uncomfortable. But when your seated in First Class you have a seat that you could lean back and relax, you get served your food(good food at that!!) and some first class seats have been arranged to where it can be converted into a bed.

Now take that into the spiritual realm. When you have a "Coach" mentality you settle for anything, you never strive to go beyond where you are. You believe that where you are right now is it. So if you're struggling financially, or in your relationship you feel that the sum total of your life.

But when you have a "First Class mentality" you believe what God says that you're a royal priesthood, and a chosen generation. You believe for the best, you strive for the best; you're not moved by external circumstances because of the inward truth residing on the inside of you.

This place of being seated in Christ encompasses three things:

(1*) Its a place of Authority*

"Behold I have given unto you Power (Authority) to tread upon serpents, and scorpions and over all the power of the enemy, and nothing shall be no means harm you"(Luke 10:19)

(2) ***Its a place of Rest***

"Come unto me all ye that labor and are heavy laden, and I shall give thee Rest" (Matthew 11:28)

(3) ***Its a place of Praise***

Where our relationship with the Lord grows, our fears, worries, depressions are placed under his feet. For in "His Presence is fullness of joy" (Psalms 16:11)

So if you feel like you've been living in "Coach" change your seat and move up to "First Class" because you are blessed and Highly Favored of God.

DAY 25
Today's Topic Stimulus
Scripture Reference: Isaiah 48:17

Success Quote: "***When anything pushes against you, choose to let it push you up. Every occasion is your occasion to brightly shine" Ralph Marston***

As the children of God we should rejoice that we're not moved by what the economy does because God has designed a Stimulus package for us. The word Stimulus is defined in the Webster's Dictionary as "Something that encourages an activity or a process to begin increase"

For the believer here is God's Stimulus plan for you:

(1) ***His Promises***

"If ye be Christ then are ye Abraham seed and heirs to the promises"

Because you are a new creation in Christ Jesus, the blessing that was upon the descendants of Abraham now belongs to you. I called it F.B.I which is Favor, Blessing, and Increase.

(2) ***His Provision***

"The Lord will guide you always, He will satisfy your needs" (Isaiah 58:11) "As long as the earth remained there will be seedtime and harvest" (Genesis 8:22)

God has promises that no matter what situation we may encounter He will provide for His Children.

(3) ***His Protection***

"The name of The Lord is a Strong Tower, the righteous run to it and they are safe" (Proverbs 18:10)

"Thou O Lord art a shield for me, My Glory the Lifter of My Head (Psalms 3:3)

Even in the midst of any trouble God's hand of protection is upon His children. You are In Good Hands!!

With a Stimulus plan such as this it should motivated us to do three things:

(1) Keep on Praying- Your breakthrough is just a pray away!!
(2) Keep Pressing-There's something beyond your storm
(3) Keep Praising-God inhabits the Praises of His People!!

DAY 26

Today Topic: Life Lesson (PT II)
Scripture Reference: Colossians 2:7

Success Quote: **"Life is a never ending school of learning" Mark Dudley**

A few weeks ago I wrote "Life Lessons" and I share how I had studied for a test, but still failed. I had failed to study the entire material which caused this failure.

Today I took the test again after two weeks of intense studying and this time I pass (81%) and I give God all the Glory.

As I shared previously there is a life lesson to be learned in every situation good or bad. Our trials and circumstances may seem difficult at the time, but going through them strengthen our dependence on God.

After this test was finally over I learned five very important Life Lessons that I pray will bless you:

(1*) Never Give Up*

"I will bless the Lord at all Times and His Praise shall always be in my mouth (Psalms 34:1)

"Bless the Lord; O my soul and all that is within me bless His Holy Name"(Psalms 103:1)

(2) ***Persistence Pays Off***

"And let us not be weary in well doing, for in due season we shall reap if we faint not" (Galatians 6:9)

"Thou therefore endure hardness, as a good solider of Jesus Christ" (2 Timothy 2:3)

(3***) Never short-change yourself***

"I can do all things through Christ that strengthens me" (Phil. 4:13)

"The Lord is on my side; I will not fear: what can man do to me?

(Psalms 118:6)

(4) ***Study everyday whatever will help you to succeed***

"Study to show thyself approved unto God"(2 Timothy 2:15)

"Thy word is a lamp unto my feet and a light unto my path" (Psal ms 119:12)

(5) ***You're smarter than you think***

"Ye are God's workmanship created in Christ Jesus unto good works"(Eph 2:10)

"Let this mind be in you which was also in Christ Jesus".

DAY 27

Today Topic: Kingdom-minded Lifestyle
Scripture Reference: Matthew 6:33, Romans 14:17

Success Quote: **God put me on Earth to accomplish a certain number of things. Right now I'm so far behind I will never die! "Anymonus**

During his three and half year ministry Jesus was always mentioning the Kingdom of God. And he not only preached about it, but he showed it. He not only reached out to the Jews but also to a Samaritan woman. Many times his own disciples who tried to tell Him that they had no dealing with certain people like the three lepers that cried out for their healing, or the woman who considered herself "a dog" but felt that she was worthy enough to eat crumbs from the master's table, but Jesus still reached out to them.

Jesus was Kingdom-minded. He declared that He did not come to call the righteous, but sinners to repentance. We see this Kingdom mindedness in the Garden of Gethsemane when He said to His Father "Not my will but yours be done".

We must have the same Kingdom minded lifestyle that Jesus had. I know that some of us may be struggling in our finances, in our relationships, or on our jobs but while we are crying out to God for our breakthrough lift up someone else who may be going through the same thing or even worse.

I desire to see you prosper in every area. I want your life to be an example to the world how God takes care of His children.

So in your prayer time pray for someone you may know who needs God's divine intervention in their lives. For what you make happen for others God will make happen for you!!

DAY 28

Today's Topic: Push
Scripture Reference: James 2:17

Success Quote: **"The best job goes to the person who can get it done without passing the buck or coming back with excuses." Napoleon Hill**

Something very interesting happened on Sunday at the church I attend. We had a guest musician who led praise and worship along with the other singers. During the praise and worship portion of the service he was singing at a level the other singers were not too familiar with. On each song he was imploring the other singers to step up and sing higher. The singers responded by singing at the same level they were used to singing

My Bishop commented that "He was pushing them" and they were not prepare for the "push" so they stayed in their comfort zone.

How many of us can be honest with ourselves and say we've stayed in our comfort zone too long. It's good to have someone come along and "push" you to do more, and to stretch your "Faith muscle".

In the above scripture it reads "Faith without works is dead" or "Faith without corresponding action to back it up is void and unable to produce it's desired result" in other words you have to put some feet to your faith.

Stuff won't just happen for you, you have to do something. You have to be willing to go outside your comfort zone to experience something you have never experience before.

There's an incident that happened in the New Testament with Jesus and Peter who was on the boat. Peter saw Jesus walking on the water and said "Lord if it be, bid me to come", and Jesus answered "Come". Now it was Peter's responsibility to respond to the words of Jesus and get out of the boat.

I believe the Lord is speaking that same word to many of us. We heard His word many times and we have the understanding that God desires us to live a successful life. Now we have to "push" ourselves and begin to move towards that which we desire.

All the promises, and blessings of the Lord are available for us, but we have the responsibility to not pray about it but "push" ourselves to have what belongs to us!!

DAY 29

Today's Topic: The Difference Maker
Scripture Reference: Luke 10:19

Success Quote: **"What lies behind us, what lies before us are tiny matters compared to what lies within us" Ralph Waldo Emerson**

For a moment ponder the above quote, and think about where you are, and where you desire to be. All of us have a past, some good and some bad but the thing to remember is this: It's your past. That's what behind us.

In front of you is the plan of God outlined in the scriptures John 10:10, Jeremiah 29:11 and, Ephesians 1:2.

Joshua 24:15 God says "Choose ye this day whom ye shall serve, so God leaves the choice to you and me.

You are the difference maker. Success or failure is up to you. We know the economy is bad, and people are losing their jobs but according to the Word of God it is God who gives us the power to get wealth, but it <u>our</u> responsibility to always remember and give God the glory for the things He has done.

Back to the above quote, 2 Timothy 1:7 declares that God has not given us the spirit of fear, but He has given unto us love, power, and a sound mind. The opportunity to fear, be anxious and concern will always be behind us, and in front of you, but the difference is our allowing the Spirit of God to lead us and guides us into all truths.

What lies within you is greater than any problem or circumstance. God has given you and me the capacity to overcome and to conquer every situation.

Be the Difference maker in your family, on your job, in your church and in your community always remembering "This is the Lord's doing and it is marvelous in our eyes".

DAY 30

Today's Topic: The Ball is in your Court
Scripture Reference: James 2:17, Deuteronomy 30:19, Isaiah 1:19, John 3:16

Success Quote: ***"Every Decision creates Increase or Decrease"*** Mike Murdock

All of the above scriptures deal with a decision and the consequences that go with it. We can choose life, and blessing or we can choose curses. We can be willing and obedient or we can rebel. Each time we make a decision whether good or bad it sets in motion two laws: The Law of Increase, or The Law of Decrease.

In Mark 11:24 Jesus said when ye stand praying forgive that your Father may forgive you your trespasses.

I think all of us have been offended by someone, whether it was a close friend, family or church member. We can choose to take the offense and allow that offense to hinder our growth in the Lord (decrease) or we can choose to forgive which is an indication of our maturity in God (increase).

All of us in the church have heard every scripture on giving, but the decision to give or not to give is totally up to us; notwithstanding if we choose to give God will open up the windows of heaven, but if we choose not to give we live under a closed heaven financially (You have put seed in the ground to receive a harvest)

The issues of life whether it's health, finances, or family will always surround us, we can choose to let the issues deal with us or we can using the principles of God's word deal with the issue.

The Ball is in your court. What are you going to do? I believe we should take the stand that Joshua took when he said "As for me and my house we will serve the Lord".

I choose to live in the blessing of the Lord. I choose to have the life of God flowing in my life in every area. What is your choice?

DAY 31

Today Topic: Dare to Be
Scripture Reference: 1 Samuel 17:1-18

Success Quote: **"You've got to be before you can do, and do before you can have" Zig Ziglar**

There's a point in the 17th chapter of Samuel that I want to point out to you. We know that this is the encounter that David had with this giant Goliath. Before David came on the scene Goliath was defying the armies of Israel day and night for forty days. Now defying means he was daring them to come against him. This great army was in fear of this man who didn't raise a sword but just spoke fear into them.

Now the Bible declares that the devil walks about as a roaring lion seeking whom he may devour. I look up the word devil in the Greek dictionary and the word they used for devil is diablo and the definition of diablo is "someone who keeps coming at you hurling false accusations until it's penetrates your mind".

Think of about, the devil is defying you each and everyday daring you to believe God's word when the circumstances seemed to be contrary to what His Word declares.

He screams at you: "I dare you to trust God for your healing". "Look what you've done, no one saw you but God saw what you did."Look at you, you brought your tithes and you're still broke. And I'm sure you can put your own spin to the negative stuff the devil been trying to feed your mind.

You respond to the devil negative words the same way David responded when he confronted Goliath. Goliath laughed when he saw this young man coming towards him. He said a few words, but after David answered him you don't read about Goliath saying anything else.

That's how you answer the devil. You dare to stand on the Word of God. You find scriptures pertaining to the thing you're believing God for and stand on it. You may have to read it a few times everyday, but hold fast to your profession of faith.

Dare to be the person that is not ashamed of the gospel, for it is the power of God unto salvation. ***Dare to be*** to person who gathers all the prayer warriors in your community to pray against all the drug dealers and gang violence that is killing our young people. ***Dare to be*** the person who starts a business when everyone says "We're in a recession". ***Dare to be*** the person who declares "By His stripes I am healed". Dare to ***be*** the one who declares "My God is supplying all my needs

Day 32

Today Topic: What are you looking for?
Scripture Reference: Proverbs 29:18, Habakkuk 2:2

***Success Quote:* "Great things are not done by impulse, but by a series of small things brought together." Vincent Van Gogh**

I was in the bookstore looking at John C. Maxwell book on the "Laws of Leadership," and one of the Laws he mentioned was The Law of the Picture which says "People do what People see".

The reason many people don't get answers from God is the same reason a thief doesn't find the policeman: He's running away. How we position ourselves to receive makes all the difference.

If you look at life the wrong way there is always cause for alarm. What you see depends mainly on what you look for. Most people complain because roses have thorns. Instead be thankful that thorns have roses.

Position yourself to receive not resist. How you see things on the outside depends on how things are on the inside of you!!

"Any fact facing us is not as important as our attitude towards it, for that determines our success or failure" (Norman Vincent Peale). "You and I do not see things as they are. We see things as we are" (Herb Cohen)

See success when others see only failure. Expect something good to happen. That expectation will energize your dreams and give them momentum. You'll often find that life responds to your outlook. We go where our vision is. What you see determines how you feel, how you act, and what you are willing to change.

Look at your circumstances from the perspective of God's word that "All things are working together for my good", so whatever I might be going through is preparing me for the next level God is taking me.

DAY 33

Today Topic: Separation
Scripture Reference: 2 Timothy 2:14

Success Quote**: "Everybody says they want to be free. Take the train off the tracks and it's free-but it can't go anywhere" Zig Ziglar**

Separation-to get or keep apart
Michael Jackson passing, Farrah Fawcett passing, The War in Iraq, The economy is still in recession. Every day we are inundated with these Headlines either on television or in the newspapers, and if you're not careful these things will hinder you from reaching your destiny in the Lord. I believe sometimes we need to separate ourselves and get so full of the Word That these things won't affect us, and we can continue to move forward.

In the New Testament many times during his ministry Jesus would separate Himself from people and his own disciples just to spend time with His Father, now of course we're not saying we should go up to the mountain top and ignore what is going on but we shouldn't allow the affairs of this life block our growth in the Lord; Yes there is a recession happening, but we're not recession-minded. We have the mind of Christ and we think on those things according to Philippians 4:7-8. Yes people are losing their jobs, and their homes, but God is our ultimate source so we look to the hills from which cometh our help.

So in spite of what may be happening in your life separate yourself to the fact That God is bigger than any situation you may be facing and He will make a Way out of no Way for You!!

Day 34

Today Topic: All Access Pass
Scripture Reference: Ephesians 2:18, Romans 5:2

Success Quote: **"I can't believe that God put us on this earth to be ordinary." Lou Holtz**

Anyone who has watched the commercial advertising "Six Flags" noticed they have what is called "An All Season Pass" which means for one price you can enjoy all the rides that are available in the park.

For the born-again believer we have an "All Access Pass" that was bought and paid for by the Lord Jesus Christ. The above scriptures tell us this access has its benefits. We can access the "grace" of God. Now grace is God's unmerited favor, and we know that favor is more important than money. With God's favor working in your life you won't have to look for money because money will be looking for you.

The Favor of God will open doors for you that may have looked impossible. The Favor of God will bring you before the people you need to fulfill the destiny in your life. But grace is also defined as "spiritual strength"; we have strength to endure any and every situation that comes up against us.

This All Access Pass allows us to come before the Throne of Grace to cast all our cares, concerns, and worries upon the Lord. We have don't have to look for a "word" but we can come before our Heavenly Father for ourselves and let Him speak to our hearts by the Holy Spirit.

This All Access Pass allows us to come into His presence with Thanksgiving and into His courts with praise. To thank Him for his Grace, Favor, and Strength that He has bestowed upon us.

Use your All Access Pass and enjoy what the Father has given you through Jesus Christ, which is Life and Life more abundantly

DAY 35

Today Topic: Response=Indication
Scripture Reference: Luke 17:1

Success Quote: **"Most of the important things in the world have been accomplished by people who have kept on trying when there seemed to be no help at all." Dale Carnegie**

How did you respond when you got the evil report from the doctor? How did you react when the bank turned you down for a loan? What did you do when you found out a close friend was talking bad about you. Our response to life circumstances in an indication of our level of growth.

In the New Testament there's a story of the disciples on a boat and there was a storm taking place, and the boat was tossing as the waves rages. The disciple reacted in fear, and they went to Jesus who was sleeping and said "Master, carest thou not that we perish? And Jesus arose from his sleep and rebuked the wind first and then said unto the sea "Peace be still". Jesus then turned to the ones who have seen Him do mighty miracles before and asked them "Why were you so fearful? How is it that ye have no faith"? In other words do you think I'm just going to let you perish with me in the boat with you?

Please hear me, I'm not saying it's wrong to get emotional and feel like no one understand your situation, but knowing who we are in Christ, and knowing the will of God for our lives our reaction should be "This Too Will Pass". Because I'm in the music ministry, I noticed whenever something negative happens in my life, my first reaction is singing a song like <u>"It Ain't Over, until God says it's over</u>" or <u>"Never would have made it"</u> or some song that will build up my faith in God's protection and provision. The Bible declares that "Out of the abundance of the heart the mouth speaks" which means when life situations come up against you whatever has abundance in you will flow out of you whether its faith or fear.

Beloved, when things happen in your life let your reaction be an indication that "No weapon formed against you will prosper", and that "All things are working together for my Good", and no matter what it may look like God is going to get the Glory out of this!!

DAY 36

Today's Topic: The Father's Love
Scripture Reference: Romans 8:15

Success Quote: **"Life in abundance comes only through great love." Elbert Hubbard**

Millions of people watched Michael Jackson's daughter's tearful speech. Her describing how from the first day she was born her "Daddy" was the best Father she knew brought tears to the thousands who were assembled in the Staples Center. In spite of all the news media had reported about her father, nothing could replace the love she had for him. It was truly a moving moment, one that no one will forget.

Think for a moment the Love your Heavenly Father has for you and me. He loved us even when we were unlovable. He showed His love for us when he gave his only son Jesus to die on a cross for our sins, because He wanted to establish that close relationship He had with man before the fall in the Garden of Eden.

Your Father loves you so much that He doesn't look at you as a mistake, or failure. He looks at you as His child fearfully and wonderfully made in His image. Think of the time that it should have been you in that car accident, or some other terrible circumstance and Your Father protected you and kept you safe.

The Father's Love is so awesome that He takes all our sins, and cast them into the sea of forgetfulness, and He remembers your sins no more. Psalm 35:27 declares that The Father gets pleasure when we prosper. Our Father enjoys seeing us prosper in every area, because it's represent who He is, and He is Great and Greatly to Be Praised.

So as we remember the words of Paris Michael Katherine Jackson, let us remember Our Father who said He will never leave nor forsake us!!

DAY 37

Today Topic: Forget Not!!
Scripture References: Psalms 103:1-22, Hebrews 2:1

Success Quote**: "You can do what you have to do, and sometimes you can do it even better than you think you can." Jimmy Carter**

I was in prayer asking the Lord what I should share with you, and Psalms 103:1-22 came up strong in my spirit. I started looking at it and the two words that stood out to me was "Forget Not". With all that's happening in the world (the economy, the war in Iraq) and what is now taken place in the church (false teaching) it's refreshing to remind ourselves of the many wonderful benefits the Father has given unto us.

(1) ***He has forgiven all our sins***

God doesn't just forgive our sins, but He cast them into the sea of forgetfulness. People will try to remind you of what you've done and try to label you based on you've done. But when you confess your sins He Is Faithful and Just to forgive!!

(2) ***He Has Healed All Our Diseases***

No matter what dis-ease it may be (stress, worry, doubt, unbelief) along with the other dis-eases by the stripes of Jesus you are healed and you are whole. If you're sick right lay your hands on yourself and asked that healing power of Jesus flow through your body.

(3) ***He Has Redeemed Us from Destruction***

Jesus said "Peace" which is undisturbed well-being has he given unto us. We have peace when everyone else is discouraged, and dismayed, and uncertain about their future. We know that the plan of God is for us to prosper and be in good health.

(4) ***He Has Crowned Us***

Think about that. The Lord has crowned you and I with loving-kindness and tender mercies. He loves us in spite of what we've done, and where we've been, and He has shown us His tender mercies in that when everyone else has given up on us God looked beyond our faults and saw our needs!!

So "Forget not" the benefits the Father has given you through Jesus Christ. Rejoice in the knowledge that you've been forgiven, healed, redeemed and crowned by Almighty God!!

Day 38

Today's Topic: Proper Alignment
Scripture References: Matthew 6:33

***Success Quote*: "Develop the winning edge; small differences in your performance can lead to large differences in your results." Brian Tracy**

I was watching an infomercial and they were talking about back pain, and foot problems. They had this doctor who explained that when one part of the body is out of alignment it affects the entire body. I thought about this and that statement rings so true when it comes to things of God.

We have to be in proper alignment in order to receive God's best in our lives. No, I'm not saying you have to be perfect, but you should be striving to be more mature in your daily walk with Christ.

In Romans 10:9-10 it says to be saved you have to **confess** with your mouth the Lord Jesus and **believe** in your heart that God raised Jesus from the dead.

In Matthew 7:7 it says in order to receive answers to your prayers you have to ***ask, seek,*** and ***knock*** before the door is opened.

In Mark 11:23 the Word of God declares that I can speak to any mountain in my life if I ***believe*** and ***not doubt in my heart***.

In Malachi 3:10 before God opens the windows of Heaven, we have to ***bring*** (not pay) the tithe into the storehouse.

Everything has to function in alignment with the Word of God because God is a God of order. Before I can receive ***forgiveness*** I must ***forgive.***

If I lack wisdom I can ask of God, but I must ask in ***faith*** without ***doubting.***

Think about an orchestra. They have to perform in front of thousand of people who are lovers of classical music. If one note is off line the conductor would know, the audience would know and the other musicians would know because it would distract them.

So it is with us, we have to do a daily checkup on yourself to see if we're in ***proper alignment*** with the will of God in our lives because we want nothing to stand in our way of receiving God's best!

DAY 39

Today Topic: How far will you go?
Scripture References: James 1:12, 2 Timothy 2:3

Success Quote: **"People of mediocre ability sometimes achieve outstanding success because they don't know when to quit. Most men succeed because they are determined to." George E. Allen**

In the book of Joshua God speaks to Joshua and tells him to have the Israelites walk around the walls of Jericho seven times, and on the seventh day shout and watch the walls came down.

In the Books of 2 Kings a widow woman is down to her last meal for herself and her son. A man of God named Elijah comes to her house give her an instruction, she follows His instruction and is blessed in the midst of a famine in the land.

In the New Testament a woman with an issue of blood hears about Jesus coming through her town. She presses her way through the crowd, and touches his garment, because she said within herself "If I can touch the hem of His garment I shall be made whole" and she was healed and made whole in one day.

In light of the following scriptures we just showed you, I want to ask a question: How Far Will You Go?

Would you stand on the Word of God and believe Him for your breakthrough when it seems like nothing is happening?

Would you trust Him to take care of you when you're down to perhaps your last, or you may have lost your job or some other circumstance?

Would you continue to press your way in prayer, and praise and worship when the issues of life come against you?

Every successful businessman will tell you that they endure difficult times when they first started off, but they preserve through tough times to become as successful as they are.

So How far will you go to have God's best? Would you turn off the television and read and study the vision God has for you in His Word?

A marathon runner isn't concern if they finish first or last; just as long as they finish. They would endure the heat, the pain in their legs just to complete the race.

DAY 40

Today Topic: *Discovery*

Scripture Reference*:* Ephesians 1:17-19, Ephesians 2:10

Success Quote: **"To be a great champion you must believe you are the best. If you're not, pretend you are." Muhammad Ali**

A young man raised by a single mother, gets involved in selling drugs and gang violence. But discovers he has a love for music, especially rap music. His discovery leads him to make a record deal with a major recording company. He is one of the most well known artists today. You know him as 50 cents, but his real name is Curtis Jackson. While he was making millions selling records, he makes another discovery that leads him to get involved in marketing vitamin water which has made him a multi-millionaire.

In the Word of God, a young man named David is tending sheep while his brothers and the armies of Israel are being taunted by Goliath. When David come down to give his brothers lunch he hears the taunts of Goliath and while everyone else is afraid to confront this giant David makes a startling discovery. When He confronts Goliath, he makes a declaration that the same God that used him to defeat the lion and the bear was able to use him again to defeat this giant. And you know the rest of the story.

I pray that you understand what I'm conveying to you. Because you pray and fasted and study and mediated in the Word of God day and night you should make a life-changing discovery. You don't have to worry or be in fear, because you discovered that God has not given you the spirit of fear, but of love, power and soundness of mind. You don't have to be sick, because you've discovered that by the stripes of Jesus you are healed right now!! You don't have to worry about you know you hold tomorrow!!

The Bible declares that "Greater is He that is within me, than He that is in the world. That's a life changing word from the Lord. You have greatness on the inside of you that can overcome anything that you may encounter, but you have to discover that and then start acting like it is so.

You can start that business, because the wisdom of God will direct you and help you make wise decisions. You can have a happy home because your prayers availeth much. Nothing is impossible unto you because you discovered that God is on my side, and if God is on your side you have nothing to fear.

A Final Word

My hope and prayer is that you were blessed by the words of encouragement in this book. For everyone who ever had a dream I would say to you: Dream On.

The sky is the limit, so don't look down on yourself, or your dream.

Don't allow anything or anyone stop you from reaching your goals

I believe in you, and I know God believe in you. Now you must believe in you. Through Christ you can do all things, so there's nothing impossible.

Look at the men and women mentioned in the "Hall of Fame of Faith". They went through many difficult times, and survived. Now they are our examples.

Now it your time to be an example to someone else who feels that their dream is unattainable.

Go For It!!